Dear Baby

亲爱的宝贝

图书在版编目（CIP）数据

亲爱的宝贝 /（韩）黄珍绘；赵阳译.
—北京：北京联合出版公司，2015.10
ISBN 978-7-5502-5700-9

Ⅰ.①亲… Ⅱ.①黄…②赵… Ⅲ.①胎教—基本知识
Ⅳ.①G61

中国版本图书馆CIP数据核字(2015)第154728号
版权登记号：01-2015-4507

亲爱的宝贝

项目策划 紫图图书 ZITO®

丛书主编 黄利 **监制** 万夏

绘　　者 ［韩］黄珍

译　　者 赵 阳

责任编辑 王 巍

特约编辑 张耀强 安莎莎

装帧设计 紫图图书 ZITO®

封面设计 紫图装帧

北京联合出版公司出版
（北京市西城区德外大街83号楼9层 100088 ）
北京天宇万达印刷有限公司印刷 新华书店经销
10千字 787毫米×1092毫米 1/12 8印张
2015年10月第1版 2015年10月第1次印刷
ISBN 978-7-5502-5700-9
定价：49.90元

You are
my
Little Angel.

Don't Cry Baby

Dear Baby

亲爱的宝贝

一本神奇的孕期减压胎教涂色书

[韩]黄珍 绘   赵阳 译

I'm busy now.

All About Baby

北京联合出版公司
Beijing United Publishing Co.,Ltd.

Love

等待着心中最珍爱的人

我们见面之前，
我已经深深地爱着你。

想象着你的样子就会激动，
见到你的样子后，我会多么地爱你，
想到你就会自然地微笑。

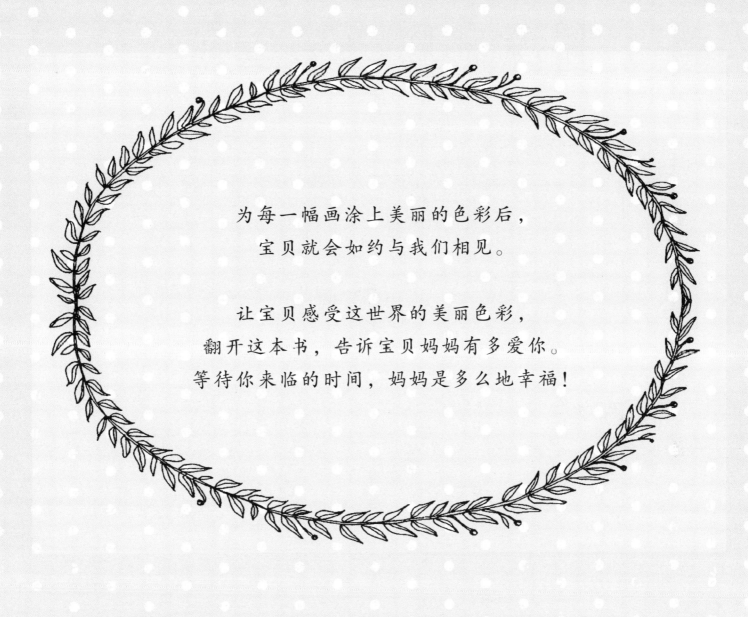

为每一幅画涂上美丽的色彩后，
宝贝就会如约与我们相见。

让宝贝感受这世界的美丽色彩，
翻开这本书，告诉宝贝妈妈有多爱你。
等待你来临的时间，妈妈是多么地幸福！

Being a mom is HARD WORK.

Things have changed.

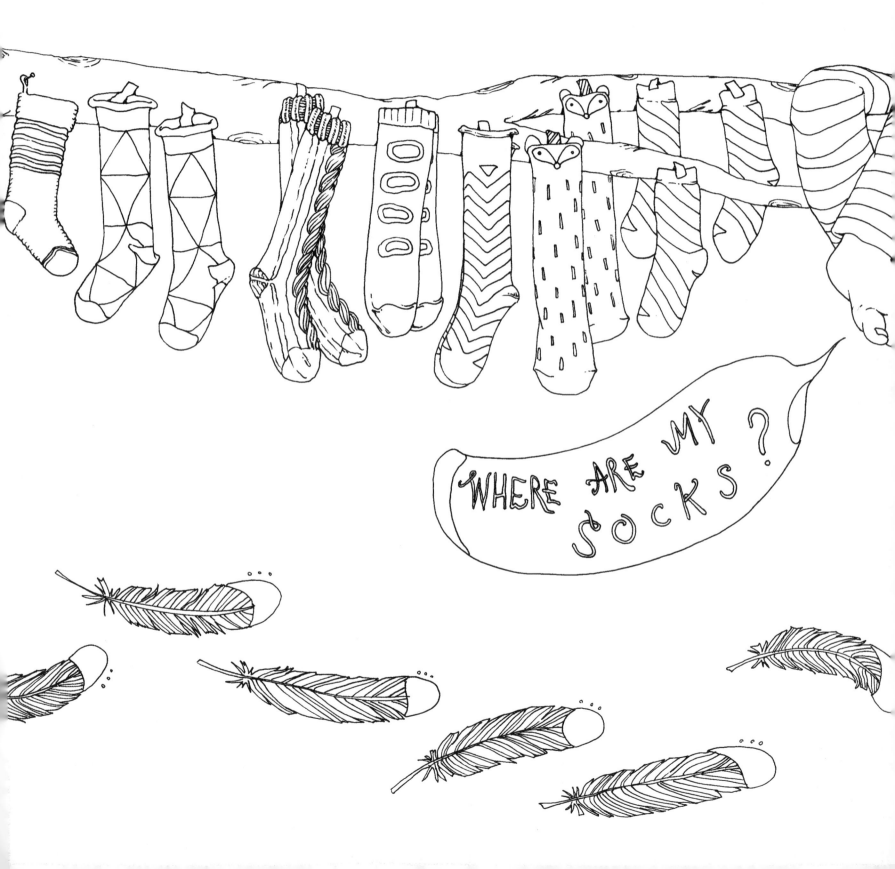

You are

my

Little Angel.

BABY GIRL

BABY BOY

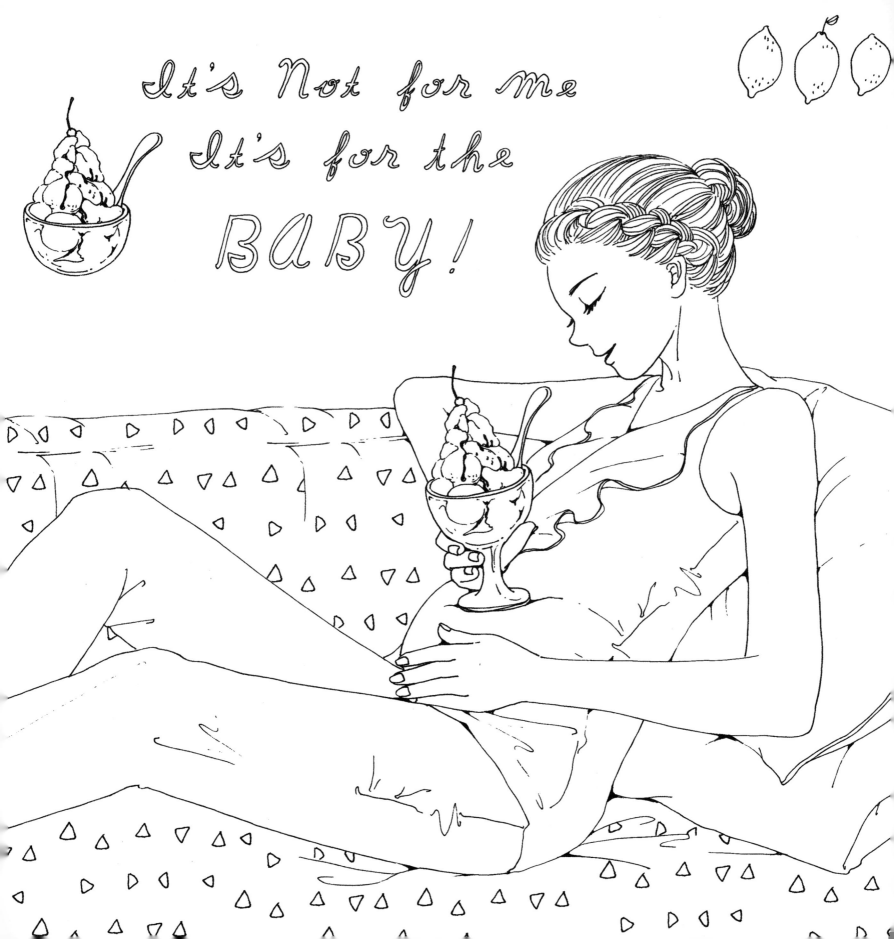

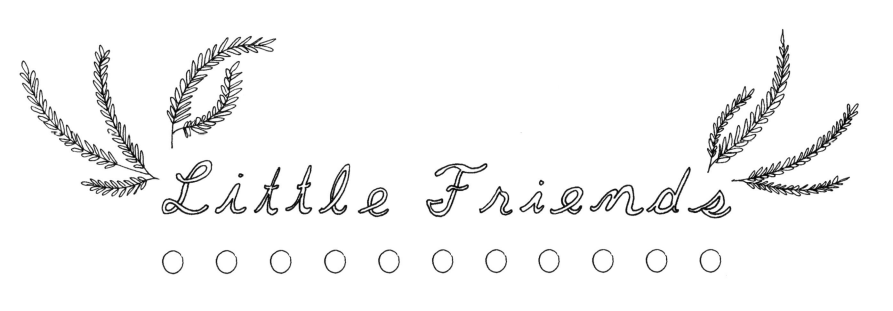

Little Friends

○ ○ ○ ○ ○ ○ ○ ○ ○ ○ ○

Sweet Dreams!

Love

Mom Needs to
Keep it
Simple.

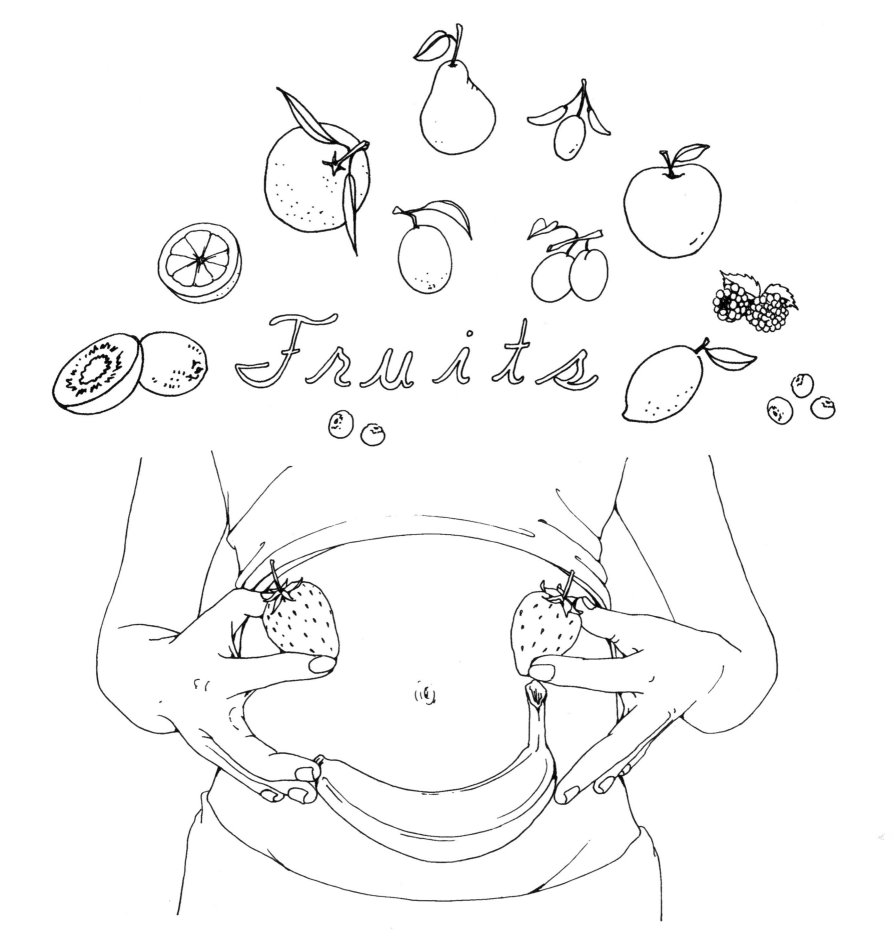

Ready for Winter

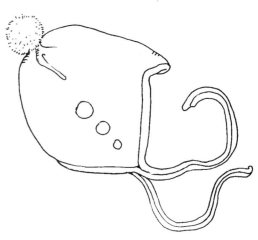

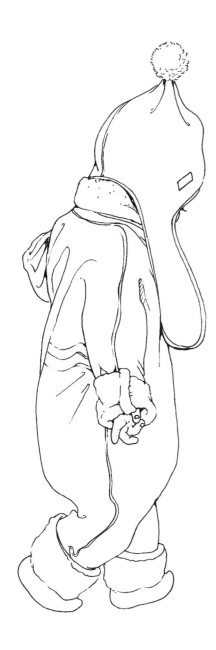

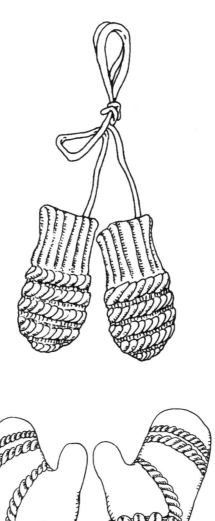

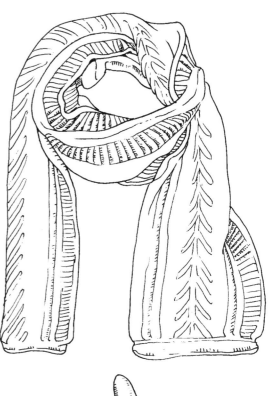

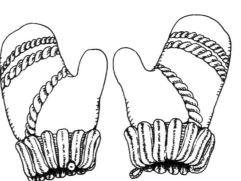

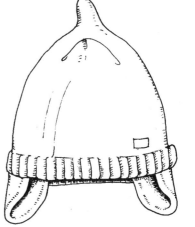

Big
not Heavy
More Pockets

BAGS

I
used to have.

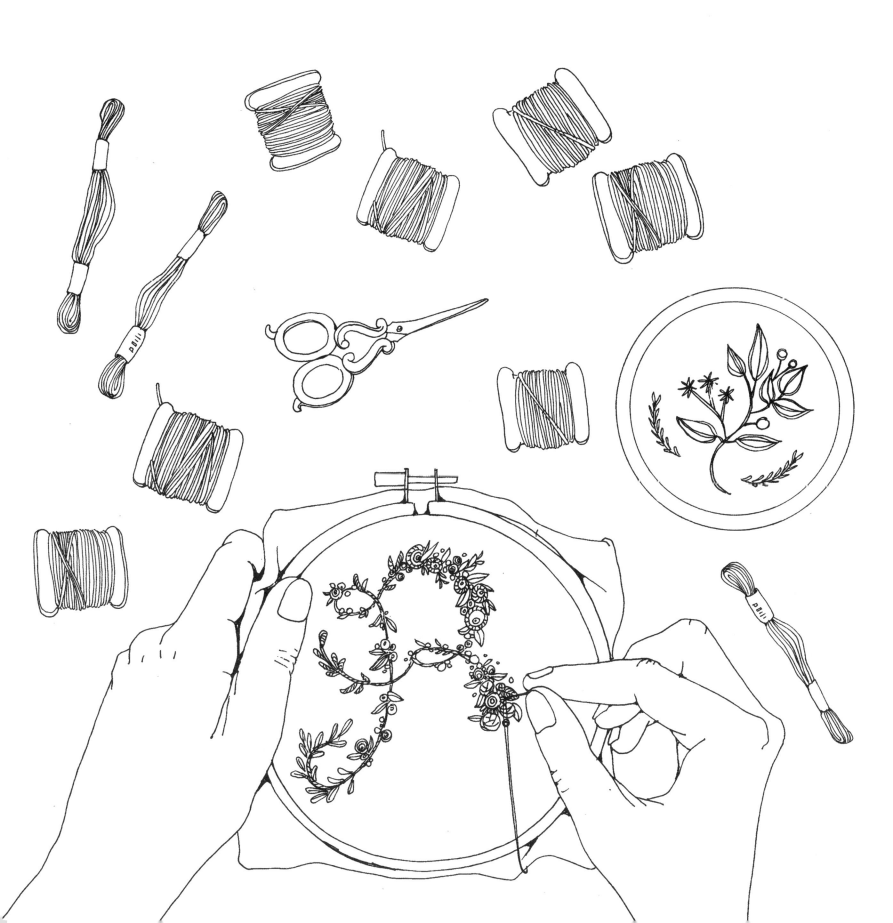

Mom.. please...

I'm busy now.

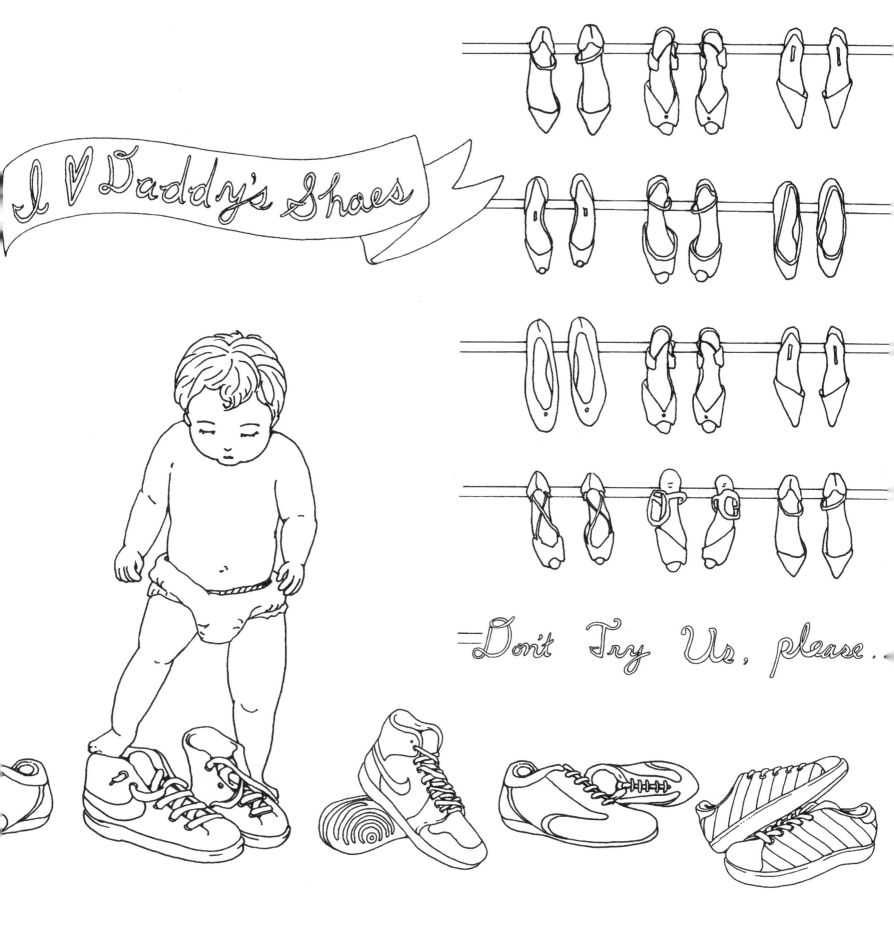

I ♡ Daddy's Shoes

—Don't Try Us, please..

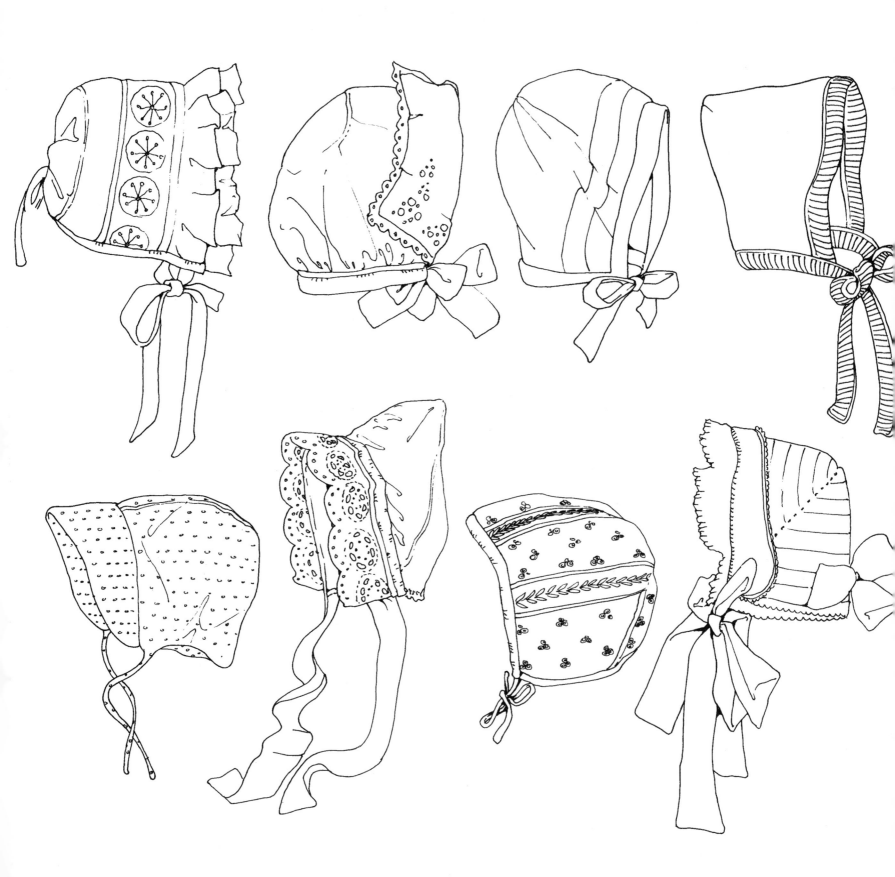

Ready for Spring

Ready for Autumn

EXERCISE after BABY!

What am I wearing today?

TWINS !

kiss to her daughter
kiss to his Wife
chu-
little kiss to her brother
Chu-

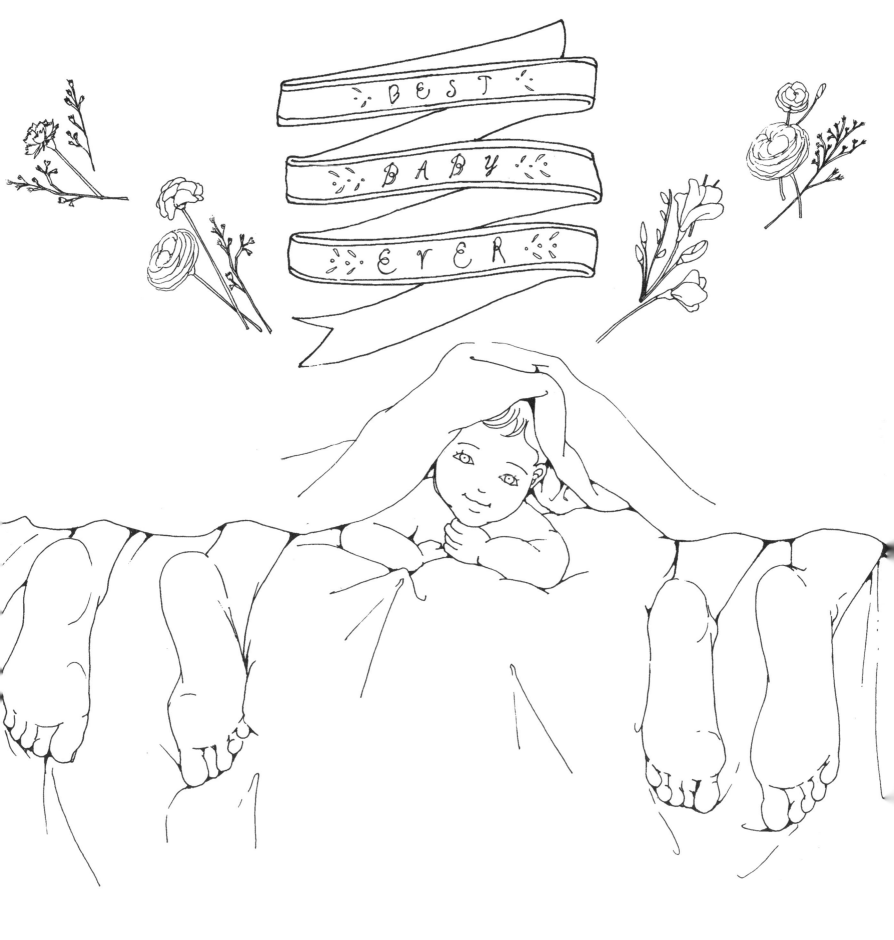

※ 涂色后沿虚线裁剪下来，放入相框中吧！

※ 涂色后沿虚线裁剪下来，放入相框中吧！

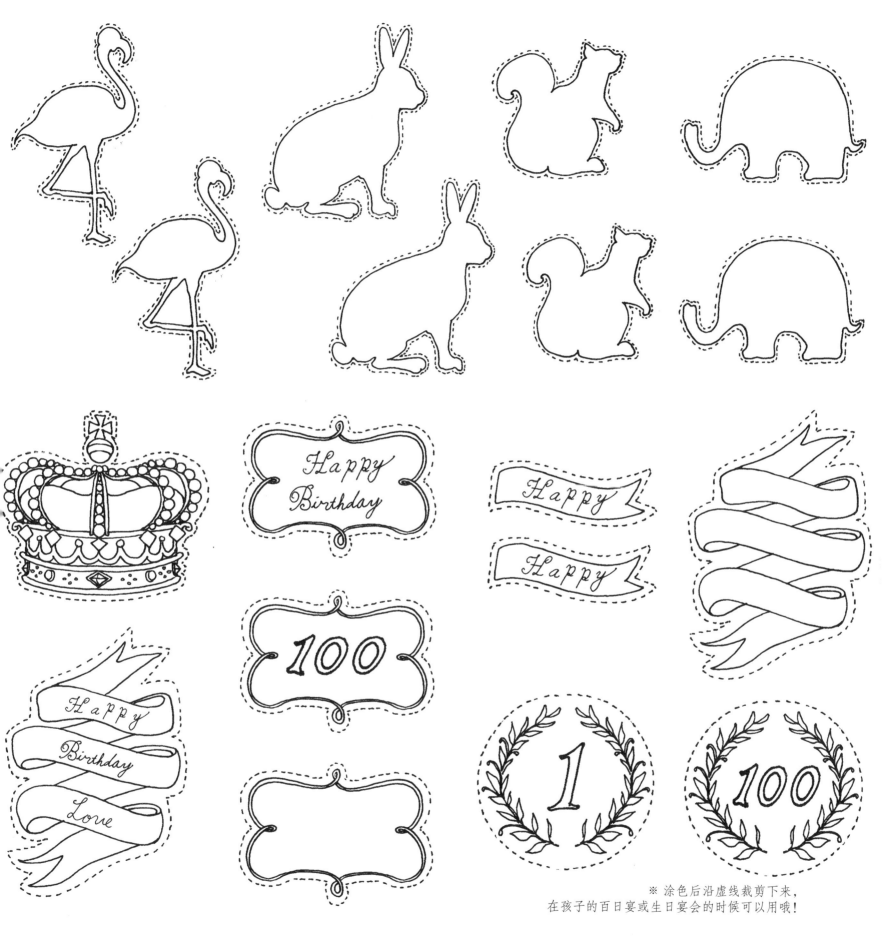

Happy
Birthday

Happy

Happy

100

Happy
Birthday
Love

100

1

100

※ 涂色后沿虚线裁剪下来，
在孩子的百日宴或生日宴会的时候可以用哦！